Native Americ in New York

Lynn George

ROSEN CLASSROOM
PRIMARYSOURCE

Rosen Classroom Books & Materials

New York

Published in 2003 by The Rosen Publishing Group, Inc.
29 East 21st Street, New York, NY 10010

Book Design: Haley Wilson

Photo Credits: Cover, p. 1 © The Mariners' Museum/Corbis; p. 4 © James Randklev/Corbis; p. 6 © Thomas Gilcrease Institute of American History and Art, Tulsa, Oklahoma; pp. 8, 16, 21 © Corbis; p. 9 © Nathan Benn/ Corbis; p. 10 © National Museum of the American Indian, Smithsonian Institution; p. 11 © Philadelphia Museum of Art/Corbis; p. 12 by Jessica Livingston; p. 14 (Jefferson, Madison) © Burstein Collection/Corbis; p. 14 (Franklin) © The Corcoran Gallery of Art/Corbis; p. 14 (Constitution) © Joseph Sohm, ChromoSohm Inc./Corbis; p. 18 © Bettman/Corbis; p. 20 © Collection of the New-York Historical Society.

ISBN: 0-8239-8401-X
6-pack ISBN: 0-8239-8414-1

Manufactured in the United States of America

Contents

St Lawrence R.

Adirondack

Lake Ontario

IROQUOIS NATIONS

Seneca

Cayuga

Onondaga

Oneida

Mohawk

Mahican

Lake Erie

Lenape

Montauk

New York's First People

New York's first people were **nomads** who arrived from the north 11,000 years ago. They hunted and gathered wild vegetables in the pine forests that covered the area.

Their **descendants**, the Algonquian, learned to plant corn, beans, and squash so they would not have to move around in search of food. They began to establish **permanent** settlements in the Hudson River valley and on Long Island around 700 B.C.

Around the year 1300, the Iroquois moved onto the land west of the Algonquian. They were soon fighting with the Algonquian and with each other for food and land, and to win honor in battle.

◀ The Algonquian groups, or nations, included the Lenape, Montauk, Mahican, and Adirondack. After moving into New York, the Iroquois separated into many nations, including the Onondaga, Seneca, Cayuga, Oneida, and Mohawk.

La pesche des Sauuages p. 15

passinassiocek Je decris cette pesche aillieur qui est une des
choses tres mervueilleusses touchand La f. 19 Pesche

kouabâgan

alticamek

Bateskoupin

eskan

Instrumens pour La pesche

6

Woodlands Society

The society of early Native Americans in New York is called the Woodlands Society. The Algonquian and Iroquois lived beside rivers and lakes, which provided fresh water and fish. They traveled the rivers and lakes in canoes made from birch bark. They also used bark to cover their houses.

Woodlands people used stone tools for many tasks. Men made sharp stone points for their hunting spears. Women used stones to grind the corn they grew. They ground nuts and seeds from the forest the same way. They also used stones to clean animal hides that would be made into clothing.

◄ Around 1675, a French explorer named Louis Nicolas drew a picture of Iroquois men fishing from a birch-bark canoe. Nicolas showed how the Iroquois used a net, spear, and other tools to catch fish. He labeled the Iroquois as *sauvages,* or "wild people," because he did not know much about their way of life.

Grasset St Sauveur inv. direx   J. Laroque Sculp

Sauvage Iroquois

8

Life in a Longhouse

The Iroquois lived in **longhouses** and called themselves the Haudenosaunee (hoh-dee-noh-SHOW-nee), or "People of the Longhouse." Several **generations** of a family lived in each longhouse. Groups of families made up **clans**.

Iroquois women owned the land, raised the crops, and made decisions for their village. Clan Mothers, the oldest women in each clan, chose the village leaders.

Men hunted, fished, conducted business, and fought battles. Young men gained strength and learned to value bravery and honor by playing **lacrosse**. The Iroquois even used lacrosse to settle disagreements between villages.

longhouse

◄ Europeans did not understand the importance of women in Iroquois society, so they made pictures mostly of Iroquois men. This 1796 picture by a French artist shows an Iroquois man dressed for war, holding weapons in both hands.

10

The Arts

The Algonquian made beautiful baskets for carrying and storing things. At first they made baskets of bark, buffalo hair, and leaves. Later they used very thin strips of wood. They decorated the baskets with different painted shapes.

The Iroquois were famous for the way they decorated clothing and moccasins. They used porcupine **quills**, which they plucked, dyed, and flattened. It took great skill and a lot of time—a month or even longer—to create just one piece of clothing. Because of this, people valued clothing decorated with quills very highly.

◀ Quills and beads decorate this pair of moccasins from around 1900. The above portrait of Oneida chief Shikellamy, who died in 1748, shows quill decoration on his clothing.

The Spirit World of the Iroquois

The Iroquois Creation Story tells that long ago the world had only water. Sky People lived in the heavens above. One day Sky Woman, wife of the Sky Chief, fell through a hole toward the water. Animals piled mud from the bottom of the ocean on the back of a turtle to create a world for Sky Woman.

Powerful spirits filled the world that the animals created. Evil spirits caused problems. Good spirits had the power to make the world right again. The Iroquois used special **ceremonies** to call on the power of the good spirits.

◀ As Sky Woman fell, swans caught her and slowed her fall. The turtle waited in the vast ocean below for the muskrat to bring mud up from the bottom of the ocean.

Thomas Jefferson

Benjamin Franklin

14

James Madison

The Iroquois Constitution

More than 500 years ago, the Onondaga, Seneca, Cayuga, Oneida, and Mohawk formed the Iroquois League. The founder was a man known as Peacemaker. A man named Hayenwatha (hy-uh-WAH-thuh) and a woman named Jingosaseh (gee-GON-sah-say) helped him.

Peacemaker created a **constitution** for the League. The constitution said that leaders from all five nations would make decisions on matters that concerned all the nations. The League could not take any action unless all the leaders agreed. Each nation had the right to make decisions on matters concerning its own people.

◀ The early leaders of the United States borrowed many ideas from the Iroquois League when they wrote the U.S. Constitution.

Neighbors

The Algonquian and the Iroquois were neighbors who often traded with each other. In return for the prized **wampum** beads made by the Algonquian, the Iroquois gave them such things as food and tools. The Algonquian and Iroquois both used the beads to make wampum belts that recorded history.

The neighbors were not always at peace, however. Around 1570, the Iroquois began a war to drive the Algonquian out of the area. The war lasted for fifty years. When the war ended, the Iroquois controlled most of the area.

◄ White and purple beads on wampum belts were arranged in patterns that helped the village's "wampum keeper" to memorize the event or treaty recorded by the belt. When someone asked a question about the event or treaty, the keeper used the belt to help him remember all the facts.

European Explorers Arrive

European explorers reached the northern Atlantic coast around the year 1500. Almost immediately, they began to trade guns, knives, and household objects to Native Americans in return for beaver furs.

The Algonquian and Iroquois fought each other for control of the fur trade. These terrible battles were called the Beaver Wars and lasted for seventy years. The guns the Native Americans had gotten from the Europeans caused many more deaths than there had been in past wars.

Europeans also brought with them illnesses that had never before existed in the New World. Tens of thousands of Native Americans died from these new illnesses.

◄ The Algonquian first met Europeans when John Cabot, exploring for England, reached Canada in 1497. By the time French explorer Jacques Cartier arrived in 1534, the Algonquian welcomed him. This picture shows the Iroquois greeting Henry Hudson, who came to explore for the Dutch in 1609.

Ondersetschreven Gekameeck en Mattehau[...]
Mattehau[...] Wilden Eckemden [...] verklaren dat
also wij aan Robbert Sanders[...] een merkelijke
somma in Boders Schilder[...] zijn aan hem
verbinden, all [...] goederen de eygendom die
wij hebben te Schaghtkoock, welcke so langhs [...]
staat [...]den tot dat wij hebben ter voll[...] [...]
voldaen, indien des eer [...]wij de bleed
Sant sal [...]men [...] koopen, so sal dito Robbert
Sanders[...] gedeelte waarde van[t] Sant, [...] [...]
dan van de [...] [...] gedaen, [...]
in kennisse der waarhijt hebben dit met ij [...]
handt ondertekend [...] den 11 [...] de Albani 16[...]

Dit [...]
geka [...]meeck [...]
Indt[...] van
Mauritanaeu[...]

Dit is het merck [...] van Mattehaes
Als Tolck van dit [...] [...]

Abram Schuyler
Abraham [...]len

Ny Present Becker Notaris Publij[...]

Record in [...] [...] of Transport [...]
held for [...] City and County of Albany [...]
[...] 100[...] [...] Day of May [...]

Colonists Bring More Changes

European colonists brought ideas that changed Native American society. Many Native Americans became

Joseph Brant

Christians. Joseph Brant, a Mohawk leader, and Handsome Lake, a Seneca leader, combined Christian ideas with their ancient beliefs and worked to get other Native Americans to do the same.

Colonists also brought the idea that people could own land. Native Americans believed that land was there for all people to use, as long as they treated it with respect. They did not understand that they would not be allowed to use land again after the colonists bought it from them.

◀ This is part of a paper that records the sale of some Native American lands in New York to the Dutch in 1686. Native Americans "signed" their names with picture characters, seen here near the middle of the page.

Reminders of the Past

The names of many places in New York remind us of the state's Native American past. Seneca Lake and Oneida Lake are named for the nearby Iroquois nations. Manhattan Island and the Adirondack Mountains are named for Algonquian groups.

There are also other reminders. Native American lacrosse has become a popular sport. Women's importance in Iroquois society inspired American women in the 1800s to seek more rights for themselves, like the right to vote. Perhaps the most important reminder is the U.S. Constitution. It might have been very different without the example of the Iroquois constitution.

Glossary

ceremony (SAIR-uh-moh-nee) An event to honor the importance of something, often with music, dancing, and prayer.

clan (KLAN) A group of families that are all related to a woman who lived before them.

constitution (kahn-stuh-TOO-shun) A system of basic rules by which a state or nation is governed.

descendant (dih-SEN-duhnt) Someone who lives at a later time than others in the family. Grandchildren are the descendants of their grandparents.

generation (jeh-nuh-RAY-shun) People in a family who are about the same age. Parents are one generation, their children are another.

lacrosse (luh-KROSS) A game in which players score points by using a long stick with a net at the end to send a ball across the other team's goal line.

longhouse (LONG-howse) A large Native American house that had a frame made of trees that was covered with bark.

nomad (NOH-mad) Someone who does not have a permanent home but moves in search of food as the seasons change.

permanent (PUHR-muh-nuhnt) Lasting a long time without changing.

quill (KWILL) A sharp, stiff hair from a porcupine.

wampum (WAHM-pum) Beads made from seashells and used by Native Americans to make belts that recorded history or honored special events.

Index

Primary Source List

Cover. Algonquian village. Hand-colored engraving by Theodor de Bry from Thomas Hariot's *A Briefe and True Report of the New Found Land of Virginia*, 1588. Based on watercolor by John White, 1585–1587.

Page 6. *La pesche des sauvages (Native Americans fishing)*. Drawing by Louis Nicolas in his manuscript, Codex Canadiensis, ca. 1675, in the Gilcrease Museum, Tulsa, Oklahoma.

Page 8. *Sauvage Iroquois (Iroquois Warrior)*. Hand-colored engraving by J. Laroque from *Encyclopédie des voyages (Encyclopedia of Voyages)*, 1796.

Page 10. Quilled and beaded Seneca moccasins, ca. 1900, in the Smithsonian Institution, Washington, D.C.

Page 11. Portrait of Chief Shikellamy, Oneida. Painting by an unknown artist, ca. 1725–1748, in the Philadelphia Museum of Art.

Page 14. U.S. Constitution, 1787; in the National Archives Building, Washington, D.C. Portrait of Thomas Jefferson, by Gilbert Stuart, ca. 1805–1807; at Bowdoin College, Brunswick, Maine. Portrait of Benjamin Franklin, by Joseph Wright, 1782; in the Corcoran Gallery of Art, Washington, D.C. Portrait of James Madison, by Gilbert Stuart, ca. 1809–1817; in the National Gallery of Art, Washington, D.C.

Page 16. Belt and string wampum, ca. 1890.

Page 20. Deed conveying land from Native Americans to Dutch colonists, 1686, in the New-York Historical Society.

Page 21. Portrait of Joseph Brant. Engraving and etching by an unknown artist from *The London Magazine*, July 1776. A copy may be found in the Library of Congress, Washington, D.C.

Web Sites

Due to the changing nature of Internet links, The Rosen Publishing Group, Inc. has developed an on-line list of Web sites related to the subjects of this book. This site is updated regularly. Please use this link to access the list:
http://www.rcbmlinks.com/nysh/nany/